CRIMCOMICS

CLASSICAL AND NEOCLASSICAL CRIMINOLOGY

KRISTA S. GEHRING

WRITER

MICHAEL R. BATISTA

ARTIST

PATRICK M. POLLARD

INKER

CHERYL L. WALLACE

LETTERER

New York   Oxford

OXFORD UNIVERSITY PRESS

FOREWORD

My upbringing was unusual. I was born during World War II in Tanganyika (now Tanzania) to a German mother, the daughter of missionaries; and an English father, a colonial road engineer. Their marriage was stormy, and when I was ten they decided to separate. My father remained working in Africa, while my mother departed for England with me and my brother and sister. In those days, before international airline flights, this required a three-week journey on a small ocean liner.

We ended up in a small seaside town in Devon in the southwest of England, where we children attended the local schools. Partly because our mother had a strong German accent, we were met with some hostility: the town we had chosen had been heavily bombed in the war because it straddled the coastal railway line to the Royal Navy's port of Plymouth. We were also treated by local children almost as alien beings because we

did not have Devonshire accents and spoke "posh." I can vividly remember being confronted by a group of older girls in the school playground who wanted to know why, if I had really been born in Africa, I wasn't black.

The contrast was also stark between the comfortable colonial life we had led in Africa and life in postwar England, where even necessities were still rationed by the government. Furthermore, we were in effect now children of a one-parent family, which despite my mother's best efforts, meant further isolation. This was compounded by the fact that soon after we arrived in England, my older sister contacted poliomyelitis (this was well before the Salk vaccine). She was first placed in an isolation hospital and later in a specialized orthopedic hospital. These were both some distance from our town, and as we did not have a car (again, unlike our life in Africa), my mother had to take several different buses to visit her on weekends. During these visits, my brother and I were left at home to entertain ourselves for the day.

Despite these trials, like any young boy, I still managed to find ways of enjoying myself. This included listening each weekday evening to a fifteen-minute radio serial (this was in the days before television) featuring special agent "Dick Barton," an ex–British Commando who saved the nation from disaster again and again. Schoolboys like me were the principal audience. Another treat was Saturday Morning Cinema, where, in addition to a film starring Tarzan or some cowboy hero, the audience, led by the organist, would sing along to favorite tunes, such as "Oh My Darling, Clementine." While in the cinema I would also munch happily on my weekly ration of sweets (i.e., candy). But above all, I looked forward each week to getting the latest issue of my comic, the *Eagle*.

Eagle was a wildly successful publication for boys that first appeared in April 1950. It was printed in full color with meticulous drawings of the highest quality. On the front page it featured "Dan Dare, Pilot of the Future," who was locked in a struggle with "the Mekon," an evil extraterrestrial being with a large green head. But my favorite part of the comic, which I hurriedly turned to every week, was the centerspread. This featured a full-color cutaway drawing of some significant piece of technology, mostly cars, ships, trains, and planes. These drawings showed details of the technology's inner components and how these all worked together. Captivated by tales of dogfights during the Battle of Britain between British Spitfires and German Messerschmitt 109s, I was thrilled whenever the centerspread featured some notable plane, but I was also fascinated by cutaway drawings of the construction of a new freeway or the operations of a coal mine. Whatever the drawing, the ways in which the technology functioned, and how everything fitted together, kept me interested for the whole week. This fascination with how things worked led me to spend innumerable hours in my early teens constructing model planes from balsa wood kits.

With this background, I might have been expected to become an engineer in later life, not a criminologist. The reason I became a criminologist lies in the British school system of the day. All children attending local government schools had to take an exam at the age of eleven (the "Eleven Plus") to see which of them would attend a selective grammar school. I passed the exam and entered the local grammar school, where most of the teachers had degrees from Oxford or Cambridge. They were always on the lookout for children to follow in their footsteps and they selected me to take an "arts" stream of subjects rather than a "science" stream, because they thought this would give me a better chance of getting into Oxbridge. But these plans did not work out. When it was time to apply for university admission, I was utterly bored by English, history, and Latin, the school subjects that I had specialized in, and I resolved to study a science at university. I found that the only science for which I could apply with an arts background was psychology, which I studied at the University of Bristol.

On graduating, I enrolled in a master's degree in clinical psychology at the Maudsley Hospital, University of London. This degree included a research component that I found much more interesting than clinical work, and when I graduated, I obtained a post as a research officer for a group of training schools for delinquent boys in the west of England. This is where *CrimComics* catches up with me. Having identified my thinking as neoclassical criminology, Krista Gehring's text and Michael Batista's drawings then tell the story of how my interests began to shift from the criminal to the crime itself. This was the result of research I undertook trying to explain why some delinquent boys absconded from training schools—that is to say, committed a further delinquent act by running away from the school. If absconders could be predicted, they might be given special treatment or training to prevent absconding.

Drawing on my clinical training, I spent three years comparing absconders and non-absconders on a large variety of variables concerning their upbringing, their homes, their schooling, and their delinquent histories, as well as their scores on a battery of psychological tests, some devised especially for the purpose. The results were very disappointing because I found very few differences between the absconders and other boys, certainly not enough to predict absconding. At the same time, however, I began to find strong relationships between absconding and various environmental variables such as daylight hours, temperature, whether or not the boy's parents had recently visited, and whether he was thrown into the company of a boy with a history of absconding. Most important of all, as Gehring and Batista highlight, I found very large differences among the 88 schools in the system in their absconding rates, which could only be due to the features of their regimes. These findings meant that whether or not a boy became an absconder was more importantly determined by situational than dispositional factors.

I could not pursue this finding in greater depth because I was offered a job in the British Government's criminological research department, the Home Office Research Unit. However, when made head of a section charged with finding new ways to prevent crime, I drew upon what I had learned at Britain's training schools: that preventing crime is not simply a matter of changing offenders, because just as important is changing the situations that provided the opportunities for offenders to commit crime. As Gehring and Batista's *CrimComics* show, this insight led to the development of situational crime prevention and the rational choice perspective.

The key point about these ideas, and this brings me back to the *Eagle*, is that they depend on clearly understanding the mechanisms or the links between opportunity variables and the motives of the offender. I identified five such mechanisms: increasing the difficulties of crime, increasing its risks, reducing its rewards, removing excuses, and reducing provocations and temptation. Just as the links between the otherwise hidden components in the *Eagle*'s cutaway drawings of machines and technology must be understood, so must the links be understood between the opportunity structures for specific kinds of crime and the motives of offenders. Without understanding these links, situational prevention can never succeed.

Lest anyone doubt the power of a comic, including the *Eagle* and this issue of *CrimComics*, to have a powerful influence on its reader's ideas, I can only appeal to a higher authority—Stephen Hawking. According to Wikipedia, he was a fan of the *Eagle* when a boy, and when asked many years later how Dan Dare had influenced him, he replied, "Why am I in cosmology?"

RONALD V. CLARKE
Rutgers University

PREFACE

Students learn in many different ways. Our current educational system typically caters to a "traditional student," one who is expected to read the assigned textbook, attend class, and take notes. Unfortunately, many students will not read traditional textbooks (or even buy them), and many may not know how to read them in a way that lets them internalize the information and learn the material. If students *do* read the material, many may not know how to underline judiciously so they can meaningfully use the underlined material to review. Finally, when they review the underlined material, they likely engage in studying practices that research has shown to be ineffective. Reading and rereading material to the point that it is memorized misleads the students into thinking they have "mastered" that material, when in actuality, they are simply learning rote facts without making meaningful connections.

By contrast, *CrimComics* presents information in a format that students may be far more likely to read, understand, and use to review for a test, because it communicates a great amount of content through images. These images and the stories they tell may make it easier for students to digest and remember the material. And although there may be fewer words in a comic book or graphic novel, the significance of how those words are arranged in relation to the artwork conveys to students the value of the information. Therefore, the images in a comic book or graphic novel should not negate its scholarly status.

Many of the same concepts covered in traditional textbooks are also found in *CrimComics*, but are presented more concisely. It should be noted that even traditional textbooks do not necessarily cover every theory in depth. Many of these textbooks truncate theories by reducing hundreds of pages of writing and research about a single theory down to a few pages (and sometimes a few paragraphs).

Comic books and graphic novels can produce as much, or possibly even more, learning compared to traditional texts. If the goal is learning, what evidence exists suggests that a graphic approach is effective. This approach differentiates instruction and can build critical reading skills. For example, some research has proposed that reading comic books and graphic novels may require more complex cognitive skills than reading text alone. College instructors across the country have adopted graphic novels and texts for their courses to facilitate learning and enhance student engagement. Examples include *Maus I* and *II*; *Persepolis*; *Still I Rise*; *Stuck Rubber Baby*; *Race to Incarcerate: A Graphic Retelling*; and *Message to Adolf*. *CrimComics* joins these and other comic books and graphic novels in classrooms, and we intend to reach students and spark their interest in criminological theory in an entirely new way.

As with any book project, *CrimComics* consumed much time and effort, perhaps more than a traditional textbook. Thinking about theory—and, in particular, trying to design a work that best conveys the theories in a visual medium—is fun. Still, with busy lives, finding the space in one's day to carefully research, write, illustrate, ink, and letter the pages of this work was a source of some stress. We were fortunate, however, to have had an amazing amount of support during these times from family, friends, and Oxford University Press. We also want to acknowledge the talents of Pat Pollard and Cheryl Wallace. Pat's talent generated the inks for this issue that provided the unique look of the artwork. Cheryl's flair for lettering allowed us to get our ideas across to the readers.

The support of these and so many other individuals has made creating *CrimComics* possible and a rewarding experience for us. We would like to thank the following reviewers: Rose Johnson Bigler, Curry College; John Curra, Eastern Kentucky University; Camille Gibson, Prairie View A&M University; Kevin Jennings, Armstrong State University; J. Mitchell Miller, University of North Florida; Maria Tcherni-Buzzeo, University of New Haven; Harold A. Wells, Tennessee State University; Jason Williams, Montclair State University. We hope that this and other issues of *CrimComics* will inspire in your students a passion to learn criminological theory.

Classical and Neoclassical Criminology

MILAN, ITALY, 1763.

IN THE 17TH AND 18TH CENTURIES, A EUROPEAN INTELLECTUAL MOVEMENT, KNOWN AS THE **ENLIGHTENMENT MOVEMENT**, EMERGED, EMPHASIZING FREE WILL AND RATIONAL THOUGHT. IT WAS HEAVILY INFLUENCED BY PHILOSOPHERS SUCH AS DESCARTES, LOCKE, AND NEWTON...AND SOME OF THE ENLIGHTENMENT'S MORE PROMINENT PROPONENTS WERE KANT, GOETHE, VOLTAIRE, AND ROUSSEAU.

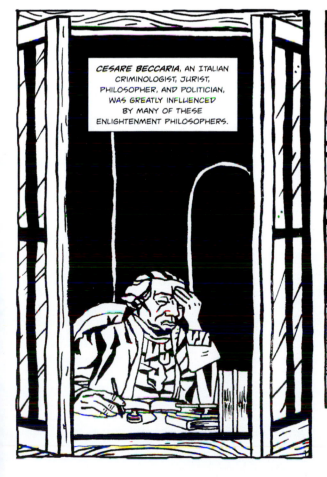

CESARE BECCARIA, AN ITALIAN CRIMINOLOGIST, JURIST, PHILOSOPHER, AND POLITICIAN, WAS GREATLY INFLUENCED BY MANY OF THESE ENLIGHTENMENT PHILOSOPHERS.

IN 1764, HE WROTE HIS TREATISE ON CRIMES AND PUNISHMENTS, WHICH WAS A CRITIQUE OF THE CURRENT STATE OF PUNISHMENTS AND THE LEGAL SYSTEM.

THESE AND OTHER IDEAS PROPOSED BY BECCARIA INFLUENCED THE FRENCH REVOLUTION OF 1789 AND THE FRENCH PENAL CODE OF 1791.

HIS IDEAS ALSO INFLUENCED THE JUSTICE-RELATED ACTIVITIES OF RULERS SUCH AS CATHERINE THE GREAT OF RUSSIA,

FREDERICK THE GREAT OF PRUSSIA,

AND EMPEROR JOSEPH II OF AUSTRIA.

BECCARIA'S WRITINGS MAY HAVE ALSO INFLUENCED THE FRAMERS OF THE U.S. CONSTITUTION.

SOME SCHOLARS CLAIM THE FIRST TEN AMENDMENTS, ALSO KNOWN AS THE BILL OF RIGHTS, MIGHT NOT HAVE EXISTED HAD IT NOT BEEN FOR BECCARIA'S EMPHASIS ON THE RIGHTS OF INDIVIDUALS IN THE FACE OF STATE POWER.

IDEAS CAUSE REACTIONS.

LONDON, ENGLAND, 1785.

CESARE BECCARIA WAS NOT THE ONLY PERSON TO BELIEVE THAT PUNISHMENT SHOULD BE A DETERRENT.

JEREMY BENTHAM, AN ENGLISH JURIST, PHILOSOPHER, AND SOCIAL REFORMER, ALSO HAD IDEAS ABOUT HOW PUNISHMENT SHOULD AFFECT SOCIETY. NOT ONLY WAS HE INFLUENCED BY ENLIGHTENMENT IDEAS, BUT HE LIVED DURING A TIME OF GREAT SOCIAL AND POLITICAL UNREST. AT THIS TIME, ENGLAND WAS EXPERIENCING ITS INDUSTRIAL REVOLUTION AS WELL AS THE RISE OF THE MIDDLE CLASS. GLOBALLY, FRANCE AND AMERICA WERE INVOLVED IN REVOLUTIONS. THESE EVENTS INSPIRED HIS PERSONAL REVELATIONS REGARDING HUMAN NATURE AND PUNISHMENT.

SAMUEL, YOU OLD COOT! HOW ARE YOU MY BROTHER?

FINE, JEREMY. I CAN SEE YOU ARE IN GOOD SPIRITS TODAY. TO WHAT CAUSE?

I'VE BEEN THINKING, SAMUEL. THINKING, THINKING!

OH DEAR. NO GOOD CAN COME FROM THAT.

NONSENSE! I KNOW YOU SAY THAT IN JEST!

I HAVE BEEN PONDERING HUMAN NATURE AND HOW THIS RELATES TO PUNISHMENT, SAMUEL.

THE CRIMINALS IN THIS TOWER, SAMUEL. WHY DO YOU BELIEVE THEY ARE THERE?

WELL, THEY COMMITTED CRIMES OF COURSE!

TRUE, TRUE. BUT FOR WHAT REASON? WHAT WAS THE CRIME TO THEM?

A MOMENT OF EVIL? AN IMPULSE?

PERHAPS. OR COULD CRIME HAVE BEEN A PLEASURABLE ACT?

SAMUEL, I BELIEVE PEOPLE COMMIT CRIME BECAUSE NATURE HAS PLACED MANKIND UNDER THE GOVERNANCE OF TWO SOVEREIGN MASTERS, PAIN AND PLEASURE.

DO YOU NOT MAKE DECISIONS THAT MAXIMIZE YOUR PLEASURE AND MINIMIZE YOUR PAIN?

OF COURSE. THAT IS COMMON SENSE.

BY THE END OF THE 1800S, CLASSICAL THEORY, WITH ITS EMPHASIS ON FREE WILL AND INDIVIDUAL CHOICE, WAS REPLACED BY ANOTHER SCHOOL OF THOUGHT KNOWN AS *"POSITIVISM."*

POSITIVISM MADE USE OF THE SCIENTIFIC METHOD IN STUDYING CRIMINALITY.

POSITIVIST SCIENTISTS BEGAN TO LOOK AT FORCES EITHER WITHIN OR OUTSIDE INDIVIDUALS THAT WERE BEYOND THEIR CONTROL AND THAT CAUSED THEM TO COMMIT CRIME.

EXAMPLES OF THESE COULD BE BIOLOGICAL CAUSES...

...OR SOCIAL FACTORS THAT MIGHT CONTRIBUTE TO WHY GROUPS OF INDIVIDUALS COMMITTED CRIME.

THESE CAUSES, WHETHER THEY WERE INDIVIDUAL DEFECTS OR SOCIAL PROBLEMS, SUPPORTED THE IDEA THAT CRIMINALS COULD BE REHABILITATED.

THESE IDEAS CAUSED REACTIONS THAT LED TO THE DEVELOPMENT OF PROBATION, PAROLE, AND INDETERMINATE SENTENCES TO SUPPORT OFFENDER REHABILITATION.

IN ADDITION TO THIS, SOME INMATES WOULD RECEIVE A BRAIN EXAMINATION TO DETERMINE IF ANY PHYSICAL CONDITION WOULD DELAY OR PREVENT REHABILITATION, WHICH WAS THE PRISON'S GOAL.

SUPPORT FOR REHABILITATION LASTED UNTIL THE 1960S...

...AND THEN ALL HELL BROKE LOOSE. IN THE 1960S, WE WERE FIGHTING IN THE VIETNAM WAR, WHICH WE WERE CLEARLY LOSING. MANY SOCIAL AND POLITICAL MOVEMENTS AROSE, INCLUDING THE ANTI-WAR MOVEMENT, THE CIVIL RIGHTS MOVEMENT, THE HISPANIC AND CHICANO MOVEMENT, THE "WOMEN'S LIBERATION" MOVEMENT, AND THE GAY RIGHTS MOVEMENT. A COUNTERCULTURE ALSO DEVELOPED WHERE COLLEGE KIDS WERE ENCOURAGED TO "TURN ON, TUNE IN, AND DROP OUT." THESE "HIPPIES" REBELLED AGAINST THE CONSERVATIVE NORMS OF THE TIME. THEY STARTED A SEXUAL REVOLUTION, USED A LOT OF DRUGS, AND LISTENED TO PSYCHEDELIC MUSIC.

LEADERS LIKE PRESIDENT JOHN F. KENNEDY, MALCOLM X, MARTIN LUTHER KING JR., AND
SENATOR ROBERT KENNEDY WERE ASSASSINATED. CITIES WERE BURNING DUE TO
RIOTS THAT RESULTED FROM TENSIONS BETWEEN POLICE AGENCIES AND MARGINALIZED
COMMUNITIES. IN ADDITION, CRIME RATES WENT UP DRAMATICALLY IN THE 1960S,
PARTICULARLY FOR VIOLENT CRIMES AND FOR STRANGER-TO-STRANGER CRIMES.

IN THE MID-1960S, LIBERALS AND CONSERVATIVES OFFERED VERY DIFFERENT EXPLANATIONS FOR POVERTY AND CRIME-RELATED PROBLEMS.

LIBERALS BELIEVED SOCIAL CONDITIONS--ESPECIALLY RACIAL INEQUALITY AND LIMITED OPPORTUNITIES FOR YOUTH--WERE THE ROOT CAUSES OF CRIME, POVERTY, AND ADDICTION.

*ANGELA DAVIS, AN AMERICAN POLITICAL ACTIVIST, ACADEMIC SCHOLAR, AND AUTHOR.

CONSERVATIVES, ON THE OTHER HAND, ARGUED THAT PRESSURES SUCH AS RACISM, UNEMPLOYMENT, LACK OF HOUSING, AND POOR EDUCATION DID NOT CAUSE CRIME.

INSTEAD, PEOPLE WERE POOR, CRIMINAL, OR ADDICTED TO DRUGS BECAUSE THEY MADE IRRESPONSIBLE OR BAD CHOICES.

GOVERNMENT CAN PASS LAWS. BUT RESPECT FOR LAW CAN ONLY COME FROM PEOPLE WHO TAKE THE LAW INTO THEIR HEARTS AND THEIR MINDS--AND NOT INTO THEIR HANDS.

IN 1968, RICHARD NIXON EMERGED AS THE REPUBLICAN PRESIDENTIAL NOMINEE WHO EMPHASIZED "LAW AND ORDER" IN HIS CAMPAIGN.

HE PROMISED TO RESTORE RESPECT FOR TRADITIONAL AUTHORITY, ESPECIALLY TOWARD THE POLICE, AND TO EXPAND FEDERAL LAW ENFORCEMENT TO COMBAT STREET-LEVEL CRIMES.

REPUBLICAN

BECAUSE OF THE SOCIAL AND POLITICAL CLIMATE, MANY CHALLENGED THE IDEA THAT OFFENDERS COULD BE REHABILITATED.

IN 1974, **ROBERT MARTINSON** PUBLISHED WHAT IS NOW AN INFAMOUS ARTICLE THAT ATTACKED REHABILITATION. THIS LAUNCHED HIM INTO THE PUBLIC EYE.

DR. MARTINSON, YOU CONCLUDE YOUR STUDY WITH THE SENTENCE "WITH FEW AND ISOLATED EXCEPTIONS, THE REHABILITATIVE EFFORTS THAT HAVE BEEN REPORTED SO FAR HAVE HAD NO APPRECIABLE EFFECT ON RECIDIVISM."

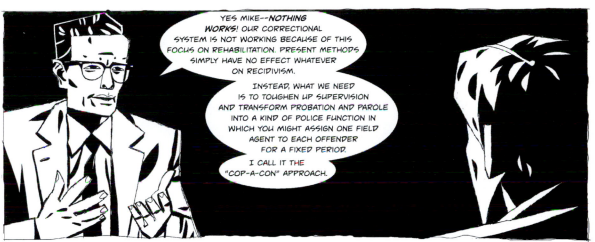

YES MIKE--**NOTHING WORKS!** OUR CORRECTIONAL SYSTEM IS NOT WORKING BECAUSE OF THIS FOCUS ON REHABILITATION. PRESENT METHODS SIMPLY HAVE NO EFFECT WHATEVER ON RECIDIVISM.

INSTEAD, WHAT WE NEED IS TO TOUGHEN UP SUPERVISION AND TRANSFORM PROBATION AND PAROLE INTO A KIND OF POLICE FUNCTION IN WHICH YOU MIGHT ASSIGN ONE FIELD AGENT TO EACH OFFENDER FOR A FIXED PERIOD.

I CALL IT THE "COP-A-CON" APPROACH.

HIS WORK WAS EMBRACED BY POLITICIANS AND INSPIRED THE ABANDONMENT OF REHABILITATION IN FAVOR OF STRONGER SENTENCING PRACTICES.

ACADEMICS, ON THE OTHER HAND, STRONGLY CRITICIZED HIM FOR DRAWING CONCLUSIONS FROM MOSTLY UNDERFUNDED PROGRAMS THAT EMPLOYED MOSTLY UNTRAINED PRACTITIONERS.

HE LATER TRIED TO REVERSE HIS POSITION IN A 1979 ARTICLE.

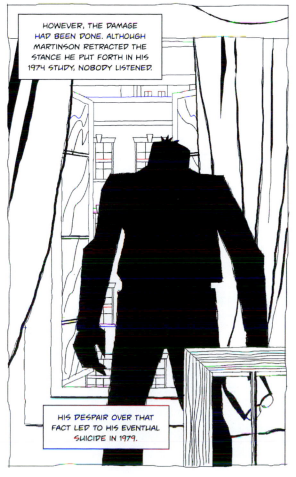

HOWEVER, THE DAMAGE HAD BEEN DONE. ALTHOUGH MARTINSON RETRACTED THE STANCE HE PUT FORTH IN HIS 1974 STUDY, NOBODY LISTENED.

HIS DESPAIR OVER THAT FACT LED TO HIS EVENTUAL SUICIDE IN 1979.

Sen. Orrin Hatch
R-Utah

ARMED WITH THE NOTION THAT "NOTHING WORKS," BOTH CONSERVATIVES AND LIBERALS CAME TOGETHER TO DEVELOP CRIME CONTROL POLICIES. CONSERVATIVES FELT THAT JUDGES WERE USING THEIR DISCRETION TO "CODDLE" DANGEROUS CRIMINALS WHO COULD NOT BE REHABILITATED. THEY FELT JUDGES WERE MORE CONCERNED WITH THE CRIMINALS' RIGHTS THAN THE RIGHTS OF THE VICTIMS. "LIBERAL" JUDGES AND PAROLE BOARDS WERE ALLOWING DANGEROUS CRIMINALS TO GO FREE TO COMMIT CRIME AGAIN.

LIBERALS FELT THAT THEY COULD NO LONGER TRUST THE STATE TO "DO GOOD." THEY FELT THE GOVERNMENT WAS CORRUPT AND NOT WORKING FOR THE BEST INTEREST OF ITS CITIZENS (EXAMPLES INCLUDED THE KENT STATE SHOOTINGS AND WATERGATE), AND THEY FELT JUDICIAL DISCRETION WAS BEING USED TO DISCRIMINATE AGAINST DEFENDANTS. LIBERALS ALSO FELT THAT THE STATE ENGAGED IN "COERCED REHABILITATION" DUE TO THE USE OF INDETERMINATE SENTENCES. IT WAS INHUMANE THAT OFFENDERS COULD NEVER KNOW EXACTLY WHEN THEY WOULD BE RELEASED, AND THEY COULD HAVE SENTENCES EXTENDED OR PAROLE DENIED DUE TO AN ANGRY WARDEN OR A CONSERVATIVE PAROLE BOARD. THE SOLUTION WAS TO ELIMINATE JUDICIAL DISCRETION AND RETURN TO THE IDEA THAT CRIME WAS A RESULT OF IRRESPONSIBLE AND BAD CHOICES.

Sen. Edward Kennedy
D-Massachusetts

THE 1980S AND EARLY 1990S SAW A RETURN TO WAYS OF THINKING ABOUT CRIME THAT REVITALIZED THE OLD IDEA THAT THE SOURCES OF LAWLESSNESS RESIDE IN INDIVIDUALS, NOT SOCIETY ITSELF.

THESE CURRENT IDEAS ARE GROUNDED IN CLASSICAL CRIMINOLOGY; THE RESURGENCE OF THESE CLASSICAL IDEALS CAME TO BE REFERRED TO AS *NEOCLASSICAL CRIMINOLOGY.*

NEOCLASSICAL CRIMINOLOGY FOCUSES ON THE IMPORTANCE OF CHARACTER, THE DYNAMICS OF CHARACTER DEVELOPMENT, AND THE RATIONAL CHOICES THAT PEOPLE MAKE AS THEY ARE FACED WITH OPPORTUNITIES FOR CRIME.

FOR EXAMPLE, *DETERRENCE THEORY* PROPOSES THAT CRIME CAN BE CONTROLLED THROUGH THE USE OF PUNISHMENTS THAT COMBINE THE PROPER DEGREES OF CERTAINTY, SEVERITY, AND CELERITY (AKA "SWIFTNESS").

MR. JOHNSON, YOU HAVE BEEN FOUND GUILTY OF DRIVING WHILE INTOXICATED.

SINCE THIS IS YOUR FIRST OFFENSE, YOU MUST PAY A FINE OF $2,000, SPEND 180 DAYS IN THE HARRIS COUNTY JAIL, AND YOU WILL LOSE YOUR LICENSE FOR ONE YEAR.

I CAN'T BELIEVE THE JUDGE GAVE ME THAT SENTENCE! DON'T YOU THINK THAT WAS A BIT HARSH?

THERE ARE STRICT PENALTIES FOR DWI IN TEXAS. A THIRD DWI OFFENSE CAN CARRY A FINE UP TO $10,000 AND 2 TO 10 YEARS IN PRISON.

SPECIFIC DETERRENCE IS DESIGNED TO DETER ONLY THE INDIVIDUAL OFFENDER FROM COMMITTING THAT CRIME IN THE FUTURE.

PROPONENTS OF SPECIFIC DETERRENCE BELIEVE THAT SEVERELY PUNISHING OFFENDERS WILL MAKE THEM LESS LIKELY TO REOFFEND IN THE FUTURE.

I WILL *NEVER DRINK AND DRIVE* AGAIN.

GENERAL DETERRENCE, ON THE OTHER HAND, IS MEANT TO PREVENT CRIME IN THE GENERAL POPULATION.

THE PUNISHMENT OF OFFENDERS SERVES AS AN EXAMPLE FOR OTHERS IN THE GENERAL POPULATION WHO MIGHT BE CONTEMPLATING CRIME.

DWI
YOU CAN'T AFFORD IT

IT'S MEANT TO MAKE THEM AWARE OF THE SEVERITY OF OFFICIAL SANCTIONS IN ORDER TO KEEP THEM FROM CHOOSING TO COMMIT CRIME.

THESE IDEAS CAUSE REACTIONS, SO MANY CURRENT CRIMINAL JUSTICE POLICIES AND PROGRAMS ARE BASED ON THE IDEA OF DETERRENCE.

$100

Price $120

JAIL

VISITING

JUST

CRIMINAL JUSTICE POLICIES SUCH AS "THREE STRIKES" LAWS, BUILDING MORE PRISONS, LONGER SENTENCE LENGTHS, MANDATORY SENTENCES, AND OTHER "GET TOUGH" POLICIES ARE ALL BASED ON THE IDEA OF DETERRENCE.

GO DIRECTLY TO JAIL

DO NOT PASS GO, DO NOT COLLECT $200

PUT PLAINLY, THERE IS A BELIEF THAT IF THE PUNISHMENT IS HARSH ENOUGH, OFFENDERS WON'T CHOOSE TO COMMIT CRIME.

ALTHOUGH MANY OF THE CURRENT POLICIES ARE BASED ON THIS IDEA, THERE IS VERY LITTLE RESEARCH THAT LENDS SUPPORT TO DETERRENCE THEORY.

RESEARCH HAS ACTUALLY SHOWN THE OPPOSITE: THAT CRIMINAL SANCTIONS INCREASE THE LIKELIHOOD OF RECIDIVISM.

COUNTY JAIL

ANOTHER CONSEQUENCE OF BASING CRIMINAL JUSTICE POLICIES ON DETERRENCE IS THAT NOW THE UNITED STATES HAS THE HIGHEST INCARCERATION RATE IN THE WORLD.

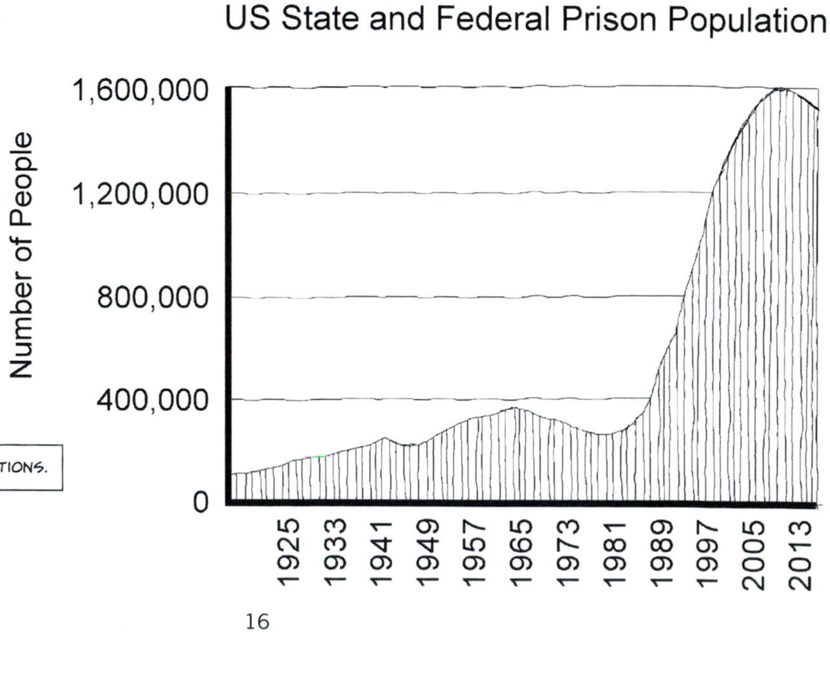

IDEAS CAUSE REACTIONS.

US State and Federal Prison Population

Number of People

1,600,000

1,200,000

800,000

400,000

0

1925 1933 1941 1949 1957 1965 1973 1981 1989 1997 2005 2013

MAUDSLEY HOSPITAL, 1965.

IN ADDITION TO DETERRENCE THEORY'S POPULARITY DURING THIS TIME, OTHER THEORIES EMERGED THAT SHIFTED THE FOCUS FROM THE CRIMINAL TO THE CRIME ITSELF.

The Maudsley Hospital

WHILE COMPLETING HIS MASTER'S DEGREE AT THE UNIVERSITY OF LONDON, *RONALD CLARKE* TRAINED AT MAUDSLEY HOSPITAL AS A CLINICAL PSYCHOLOGIST.

AFTER COMPLETION OF HIS TRAINING, HE THOUGHT RESEARCH WOULD BE MORE INTERESTING THAN CLINICAL PRACTICE...

...SO HE TOOK A JOB AS THE FIRST (AND ONLY) RESEARCH OFFICER IN THE U.K. SYSTEM OF TRAINING SCHOOLS FOR DELINQUENT BOYS.

OH MR. CLARKE, I THINK I FOUND A PROJECT FOR YOU.

SIR?

WE'RE HAVING A PROBLEM WITH BOYS ABSCONDING FROM OUR TRAINING SCHOOLS. USE YOUR TRAINING IN PSYCHOLOGY AND TRY TO FIGURE OUT WHY, WILL YOU?

YES SIR!

CLARKE SEARCHED FOR THINGS THAT MIGHT PREDICT WHICH BOYS WOULD TRY TO ESCAPE...

...AND WHAT HE FOUND WAS THOSE WHO RAN AWAY FROM THE SCHOOLS WERE NOT VERY DIFFERENT FROM THOSE WHO DIDN'T, BASED ON A COMPARISON OF A WIDE RANGE OF PSYCHOLOGICAL TESTS AND BACKGROUND CHARACTERISTICS.

WHAT HE *DID* FIND WAS THERE WERE DRAMATIC DIFFERENCES IN THE ABSCONSION RATES IN THE 88 SCHOOLS IN THE SYSTEM.

THIS SUGGESTED THAT SCHOOL ENVIRONMENTS, NOT CHARACTERISTICS OF THE INDIVIDUAL BOYS, WERE MUCH STRONGER PREDICTORS OF ESCAPES.

THIS WAS CONTRARY TO WHAT HIS PSYCHOLOGY BACKGROUND PREDICTED.

AFTER CLARKE OBTAINED HIS PH.D., HE WENT TO WORK FOR THE HOME OFFICE RESEARCH UNIT--THE BRITISH GOVERNMENT'S CRIMINOLOGICAL RESEARCH DEPARTMENT.

SEVERAL YEARS AFTER OBTAINING THIS POSITION, HE WAS CHARGED WITH DEVELOPING A PROGRAM OF RESEARCH INTENDED TO HELP REDUCE CRIME.

BY THEN, MANY STUDIES PUBLISHED IN THE U.S. AND U.K. HAD DISCREDITED REHABILITATION AS A CRIME PREVENTION TECHNIQUE.

What works? —questions and answers about prison reform

ROBERT MARTINSON

REMEMBERING WHAT HE LEARNED AT THE TRAINING SCHOOLS AND COMBINING THAT WITH INFORMATION HE HAD READ, CLARKE BEGAN WRITING ABOUT CRIME PREVENTION IN A DIFFERENT WAY.

DEFENSIBLE SPACE

Crime Prevention Through Environmental Design

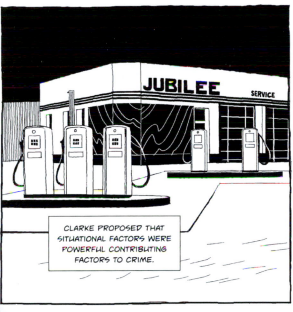

CLARKE PROPOSED THAT SITUATIONAL FACTORS WERE POWERFUL CONTRIBUTING FACTORS TO CRIME.

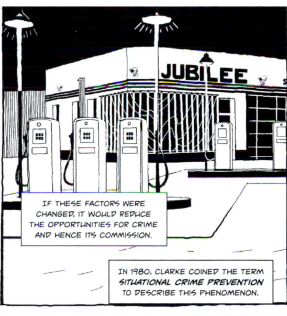

IF THESE FACTORS WERE CHANGED, IT WOULD REDUCE THE OPPORTUNITIES FOR CRIME AND HENCE ITS COMMISSION.

IN 1980, CLARKE COINED THE TERM *SITUATIONAL CRIME PREVENTION* TO DESCRIBE THIS PHENOMENON.

THERE ARE MANY TECHNIQUES THAT CAN BE USED TO REDUCE OPPORTUNITIES FOR CRIME.

WE CAN INCREASE THE PERCEIVED EFFORT TO COMMIT A CRIME, LIKE PUTTING BARS ON WINDOWS OR FENCING A PROPERTY.

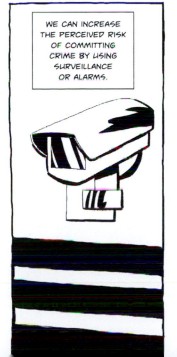

WE CAN INCREASE THE PERCEIVED RISK OF COMMITTING CRIME BY USING SURVEILLANCE OR ALARMS.

WE CAN REDUCE ANTICIPATED REWARDS, LIKE USING INK PACKS WHEN MONEY IS STOLEN...

shoplifting is STEALING

...AND REMOVE EXCUSES USED TO RATIONALIZE CRIME.

AT ABOUT THE SAME TIME IN THE UNITED STATES, ANOTHER INDIVIDUAL ENCOUNTERED SIMILAR IDEAS ABOUT CRIME.

UNIVERSITY OF ILLINOIS URBANA-CHAMPAIGN, 1976.

AS A SOCIOLOGIST, *MARCUS FELSON* WAS TRAINED TO VIEW SOCIAL FACTORS AS CAUSES OF CRIME.

Crime

CRIME RATES ARE AFFECTED BY SOCIAL FACTORS LIKE EDUCATION, UNEMPLOYMENT, AND POVERTY...

WHILE AT THE UNIVERSITY OF ILLINOIS URBANA-CHAMPAIGN, HE JOINTLY RECEIVED SOME GRANTS WITH A COLLEAGUE TO STUDY SOCIAL INDICATOR MODELS.

HEY FELSON? I'M NOT REALLY INTERESTED IN LOOKING AT CRIME, SO COULD YOU DO THAT PORTION OF THE PROJECT?

OKAY...

THE PROJECT HAD DATA FOR OVER A THOUSAND SOCIAL INDICATORS FOR THE U.S. FROM 1947 TO 1976.

THERE HAD BEEN A DRAMATIC INCREASE IN CRIME DURING THAT TIME, SO FELSON SEARCHED FOR SOCIAL VARIABLES TO EXPLAIN IT.

HOWEVER, THE USUAL SOCIAL VARIABLES DIDN'T PREDICT CRIME THE WAY HE THOUGHT IT SHOULD.

TRADITIONAL SOCIOLOGY COULDN'T EXPLAIN IT.

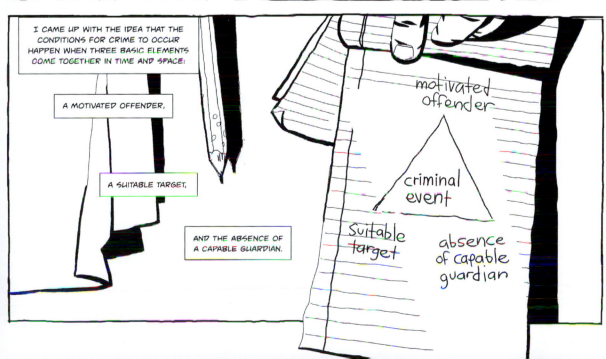

I REALIZED THAT BETWEEN 1947 AND 1976, A LOT OF OUR ROUTINES CHANGED.

HERE ARE A FEW EXAMPLES:

"THE ECONOMY WAS BOOMING, AND PEOPLE WERE SPENDING MORE MONEY ON THINGS."

"BECAUSE OF THIS, THERE WAS AN ABUNDANCE OF 'SUITABLE TARGETS.' THAT IS, MORE STUFF TO STEAL."

"IN ADDITION TO THIS, MORE WOMEN WERE ENTERING THE WORKPLACE, SO BOTH HUSBANDS AND WIVES WERE AWAY FROM THE HOME DURING THE DAY."

"THIS MEANT THERE WAS AN ABSENCE OF A CAPABLE GUARDIAN."

I CALLED IT **ROUTINE ACTIVITIES THEORY** AND AS YOU KNOW, I'VE BEEN TRYING TO PUBLISH AN ARTICLE ABOUT IT FOR QUITE SOME TIME.

I'D REALLY APPRECIATE IT IF YOU'D HELP ME REDRAFT THE MANUSCRIPT, LARRY.

OF COURSE!

MARCUS FELSON AND LAWRENCE COHEN PUBLISHED THEIR ARTICLE IN 1979 THAT PUT FORTH ROUTINE ACTIVITIES THEORY.

START

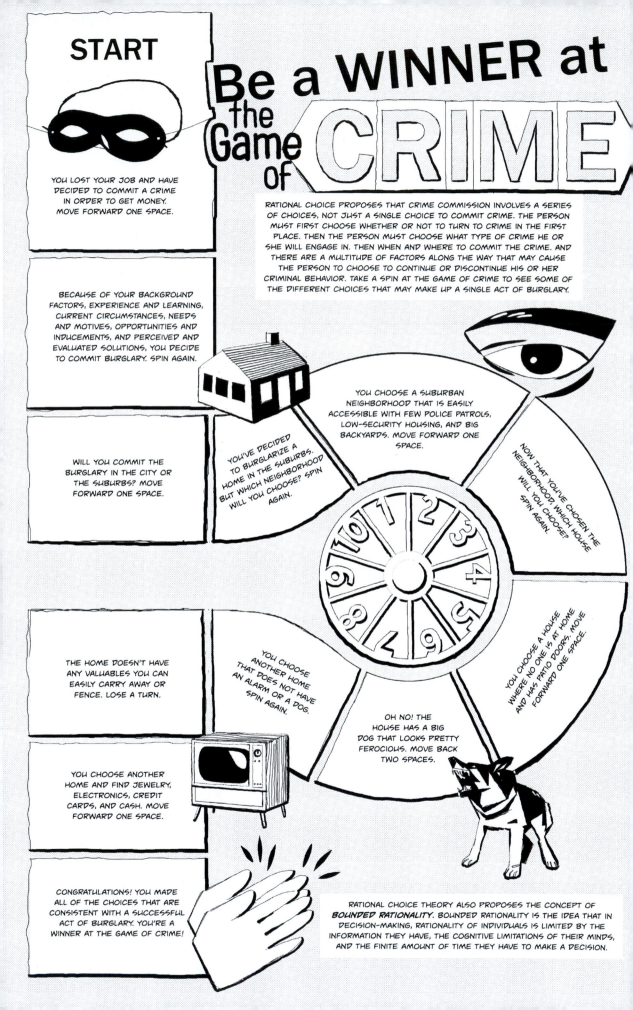

YOU LOST YOUR JOB AND HAVE DECIDED TO COMMIT A CRIME IN ORDER TO GET MONEY. MOVE FORWARD ONE SPACE.

Be a WINNER at the Game of CRIME

RATIONAL CHOICE PROPOSES THAT CRIME COMMISSION INVOLVES A SERIES OF CHOICES, NOT JUST A SINGLE CHOICE TO COMMIT CRIME. THE PERSON MUST FIRST CHOOSE WHETHER OR NOT TO TURN TO CRIME IN THE FIRST PLACE. THEN THE PERSON MUST CHOOSE WHAT TYPE OF CRIME HE OR SHE WILL ENGAGE IN. THEN WHEN AND WHERE TO COMMIT THE CRIME. AND THERE ARE A MULTITUDE OF FACTORS ALONG THE WAY THAT MAY CAUSE THE PERSON TO CHOOSE TO CONTINUE OR DISCONTINUE HIS OR HER CRIMINAL BEHAVIOR. TAKE A SPIN AT THE GAME OF CRIME TO SEE SOME OF THE DIFFERENT CHOICES THAT MAY MAKE UP A SINGLE ACT OF BURGLARY.

BECAUSE OF YOUR BACKGROUND FACTORS, EXPERIENCE AND LEARNING, CURRENT CIRCUMSTANCES, NEEDS AND MOTIVES, OPPORTUNITIES AND INDUCEMENTS, AND PERCEIVED AND EVALUATED SOLUTIONS, YOU DECIDE TO COMMIT BURGLARY. SPIN AGAIN.

YOU CHOOSE A SUBURBAN NEIGHBORHOOD THAT IS EASILY ACCESSIBLE WITH FEW POLICE PATROLS, LOW-SECURITY HOUSING, AND BIG BACKYARDS. MOVE FORWARD ONE SPACE.

WILL YOU COMMIT THE BURGLARY IN THE CITY OR THE SUBURBS? MOVE FORWARD ONE SPACE.

YOU'VE DECIDED TO BURGLARIZE A HOME IN THE SUBURBS. BUT WHICH NEIGHBORHOOD WILL YOU CHOOSE? SPIN AGAIN.

NOW THAT YOU'VE CHOSEN THE NEIGHBORHOOD, WHICH HOUSE WILL YOU CHOOSE? SPIN AGAIN.

THE HOME DOESN'T HAVE ANY VALUABLES YOU CAN EASILY CARRY AWAY OR FENCE. LOSE A TURN.

YOU CHOOSE ANOTHER HOME THAT DOES NOT HAVE AN ALARM OR A DOG. SPIN AGAIN.

YOU CHOOSE A HOUSE WHERE NO ONE IS AT HOME AND HAS PATIO DOORS. MOVE FORWARD ONE SPACE.

OH NO! THE HOUSE HAS A BIG DOG THAT LOOKS PRETTY FEROCIOUS. MOVE BACK TWO SPACES.

YOU CHOOSE ANOTHER HOME AND FIND JEWELRY, ELECTRONICS, CREDIT CARDS, AND CASH. MOVE FORWARD ONE SPACE.

CONGRATULATIONS! YOU MADE ALL OF THE CHOICES THAT ARE CONSISTENT WITH A SUCCESSFUL ACT OF BURGLARY. YOU'RE A WINNER AT THE GAME OF CRIME!

RATIONAL CHOICE THEORY ALSO PROPOSES THE CONCEPT OF **BOUNDED RATIONALITY**. BOUNDED RATIONALITY IS THE IDEA THAT IN DECISION-MAKING, RATIONALITY OF INDIVIDUALS IS LIMITED BY THE INFORMATION THEY HAVE, THE COGNITIVE LIMITATIONS OF THEIR MINDS, AND THE FINITE AMOUNT OF TIME THEY HAVE TO MAKE A DECISION.

THIS ISSUE BEGAN WITH AN INTRODUCTION TO THE ENLIGHTENMENT MOVEMENT AND ITS INFLUENCE ON CRIMINOLOGICAL THOUGHT. DURING THIS TIME CESARE BECCARIA AND JEREMY BENTHAM EMERGED AS MAJOR PROPONENTS OF THE CLASSICAL SCHOOL OF CRIMINOLOGICAL THOUGHT. THE MAIN IDEAS OF MOVEMENT ARE THAT OFFENDERS ARE RATIONAL BEINGS, HAVE FREE WILL, AND CHOOSE TO COMMIT CRIME BASED ON THE PERCEIVED RISK OF GETTING CAUGHT AND/OR BEING PUNISHED. PUNISHMENT SHOULD HAVE SOME UTILITY BEYOND THAT OF MERE VENGEANCE--IT SHOULD ALSO DETER.

WHILE THE CLASSICAL SCHOOL DOMINATED CRIMINOLOGICAL DISCOURSE FOR OVER A CENTURY, IT WAS REPLACED IN THE LATE 1800S WITH POSITIVISM, OR THE BELIEF THAT CRIME WAS CAUSED BY FACTORS BEYOND A PERSON'S CONTROL. THIS LED TO THE DEVELOPMENT OF POLICIES THAT FOCUSED ON THE REHABILITATION OF THE OFFENDER, RATHER THAN PUNISHMENT. FOR SEVERAL DECADES, REHABILITATION WAS ONE OF THE MAIN PHILOSOPHIES DRIVING CRIMINAL JUSTICE POLICIES, UNTIL THE SOCIAL TURMOIL OF THE 1960S CAUSED BOTH LIBERALS AND CONSERVATIVES TO EMBRACE MORE PUNITIVE POLICIES FOR OFFENDERS. THIS, COUPLED WITH RESEARCH THAT ILLUSTRATED REHABILITATION DID NOT WORK, USHERED IN A TIME THAT RETURNED TO IDEALS PUT FORTH IN THE CLASSICAL SCHOOL.

NEOCLASSICAL CRIMINOLOGY FOCUSES ON THE IMPORTANCE OF CHARACTER, THE DYNAMICS OF CHARACTER DEVELOPMENT, AND THE RATIONAL CHOICES THAT PEOPLE MAKE AS THEY ARE FACED WITH OPPORTUNITIES FOR CRIME. SEVERAL THEORIES EMERGED DURING THIS TIME, INCLUDING DETERRENCE THEORY AND THE CONCEPTS OF SPECIFIC AND GENERAL DETERRENCE, SITUATIONAL CRIME PREVENTION, ROUTINE ACTIVITIES THEORY, AND RATIONAL CHOICE THEORY.

Key Terms

Enlightenment Movement
Cesare Beccaria
Jeremy Bentham
Utilitarianism
Classical Criminology
Free Will
Positivism
Robert Martinson
"Nothing Works"
Neoclassical Criminology
Deterrence Theory
Specific Deterrence
General Deterrence
Ronald Clarke
Situational Crime Prevention
Marcus Felson
Routine Activities Theory
Derek Cornish
Rational Choice Theory
Bounded Rationality

Discussion Questions

Describe the difference between specific and general deterrence and provide an example of each. Give an example of a situation where there is a specific deterrent effect but no general deterrent effect.

Explain what "suitable targets" and "the absence of capable guardians" means in routine activities theory. Describe how targets and guardianship have changed in the United States since World War II.

Describe the "routine activities" in which you engage. How might these activities increase or decrease your chance of victimization?

How does a theory that focuses on why individuals commit crime differ from a "situational" theory (such as situational crime prevention)?

Think about where you live. Can you think of any changes that could be made to the environment that would make people less vulnerable to being victimized by an offender?

Suggested Readings

Beccaria, C. (1764). *An essay on crimes and punishments*. Retrieved from http://oll.libertyfund.org/titles/2193.
Bentham, J. (1780). *An introduction to the principles and morals of legislation*. Retrieved from http://oll.libertyfund.org/titles/278.
Clarke, R. (1980). *"Situational" crime prevention: Theory and practice*. British Journal of Criminology, 20, 136–147.
Clarke, R., & Felson, M. (2011). *The origins of the routine activity approach and situational crime prevention*. In F. T. Cullen, C. L. Jonson, A. J. Myer, & F. Adler (Eds.), The origins of American criminology (pp. 245–260). London: Transaction Publishers.
Cohen, L., & Felson, M. (1979). *Social change and crime rate trends: A routine activity approach*. American Sociological Review, 44, 588–608.
Cornish, D., & Clarke, R. (1986). *The reasoning criminal*. New York: Springer-Verlag.
Cullen, F. T., Agnew, R., & Wilcox, P. (2014). *Criminological theory: Past to present (5th ed.)*. New York: Oxford University Press.
Lilly, J. R., Cullen, F. T., & Ball, R. (2011). *Criminological theory: Context and consequences (5th ed.)*. Los Angeles: Sage Publications.